WILD VERGE

POEMS BY LYNETTE REINI-GRANDELL

D0107921

Holy Cow! Press
Duluth, Minnesota
2018

Cover art and author photograph by Venus deMars.
Book and cover design by Anton Khodakovsky.

Printed and bound in the United States of America.
First printing, Spring, 2018

ISBN 978-0-9986010-2-1

10 9 8 7 6 5 4 3 2 1

Holy Cow! Press projects are funded in part by grant awards
from the Ben and Jeanne Overman Charitable Trust, the
Elmer L. and Eleanor J. Andersen Foundation, the Cy and
Paula DeCosse Fund of The Minneapolis Foundation, the
Lenfestey Family Foundation, and by gifts from generous
individual donors.

Holy Cow! Press books are distributed to the trade by
Consortium Book Sales & Distribution, c/o Ingram Publisher
Services, Inc., 210 American Drive, Jackson, TN 38301.

For inquiries, please write to: HOLY COW! PRESS,
Post Office Box 3170, Mount Royal Station, Duluth, MN 55803.
Visit *www.holycowpress.org*

WILD
VERGE

For Bug (again!)

CONTENTS

5

WILD VERGE

I was skiing with my people,
but entered the cave alone.

This is the part I cannot tell you about,
I can only draw a picture of my body as something pulled me.

I was a forest mouse, and now I am stretched above the birch trees,
I am stretched above the pine trees.

My head touches the moon;
my hair is on fire with the stars.

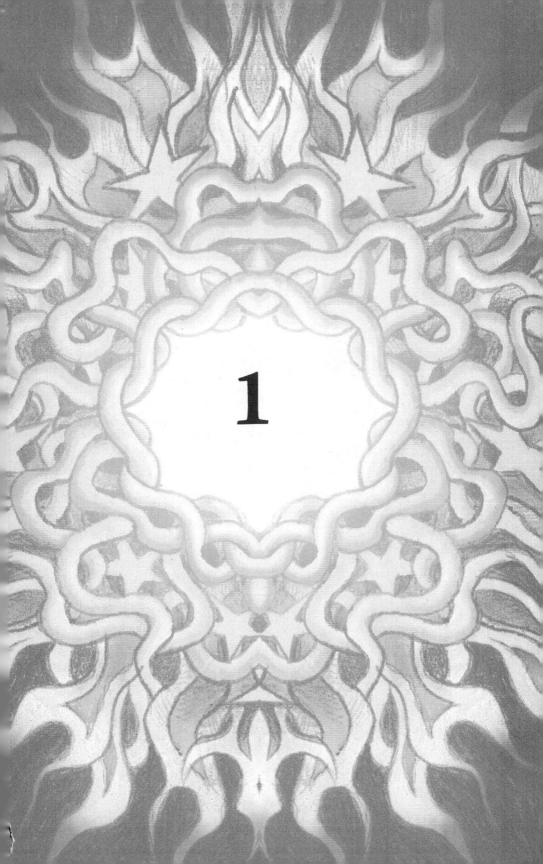

LISTENING TO SONGS OF THE FRENCH VOYAGEURS
WHILE I FLOAT IN MY MOTHER'S WOMB

I remember waking when she sang
La Claire Fontaine – clear running fountain –
then I opened my webbed fingers
and dipped them, my own paddles,
So clear I found the water
that I stopped to bathe me there.
Who could resist the songs of that great lake?

Or *Canot d'Ecorce*, my canoe of birch,
and her soprano voice inscribing hills so green
I could not see but still retained an ache for.
My favorite was *Le Voyageur*,
with minor key and three-beat circling sound
that always made me want to sing with her,
wandering the woods alone, then *si*
tu vois mon pays, if you see my country.

I wondered what that country was
where she sat at the table writing out
a melody on staves, pointing each
eighth note with its own sharp stem,
where she trimmed construction paper
and assembled the canoes.

And when she typed I heard percussive
sounds, her fingers drumming.
She might have hummed a wintering song
about working in the factory 'til spring's warmth
broke the ice. Inside her womb

I waited for her songs, her voice, the world's
clear running water, fragrant pines, the promise
of *La Rose Blanche*, pale forest rose.

FIGURATIVE BEEHIVES, LOWER SILESIA

I.

Before my mother gave me pants
long enough to tuck into the leggings
all young men strapped above their boots
in those days, before she sent me into Trebnitz forest
in my father's shirt, the sleeves reworked
but still hanging nearly to my knees
to bring back kindling, berries, forest food,
I saw human shapes in wood, their lines.

I'd finger and I'd stroke each lintel's grain,
I'd see a linden's face in bulging burl.
I masked my figure-sight obsession scouting
for the hollow trees that thrummed with honey-
birdlings. Villagers would hie me up a trunk
with smudge pot looking for the hidden
honey and the wax for evening candles.

One day old Lehrer chopped some logs and hollowed
his own roost for bees. I saw it plain
in spruce (old Lehrer's face, his firm, brimmed hat,
his beard and shoulders down to bottom button).
I begged for chisel, borrowed tools when woodsmen
stopped their sweating and they ate. They nodded
at my progress, snorted summer hop-wine
up their noses when the first bee flew
beneath old Lehrer's wood-hewn coat.
It stayed there a while.

Have I mentioned how I climbed? They sent
me up the bell-tower and I marveled
at the view, a real vision, not
of my own making. I carved a cinquefoil rose
next to our pregnant bell.
And I carved more hives to bring bees closer.

They tell me Gottfried Überschaer made hives
of twelve apostles. I could answer, have you
seen them? There is Moses, there is Simeon,
whose Bible have you read? Not that I
read well, but I get by, and I know
everyone wants three, or seven, or ten,
or twelve of something, but that doesn't make
apostles.

I know why he did it. It's best they think
we're simple and compliant. His squire tells
his priest they're holy, no harm, no foul. I hewed
my Moses the magician before he did,
and the village has been blessed. I carved
a whirling girl and my darling from
Kainowe stepped across the yard to dance.
The Prussian captains like it when I carve
a happy soldier guarding Bee and all
her flighty minions. I don't tell them it's
a charm to lead my father home. If
he can return. One man came back from Russeland.
Perhaps my father needs to maim himself
so they won't want him anymore. That's what
I did. A thoughtful tree fell on my leg

and crushed the lower half. It was better
than a battlefield. I carved new foot
and knee myself. Wood helps me dance much
better than the dead.

3.

Should I call my hives apostles? Trees
have their gospel of the earth and sky,
then they die and fill with sweetness.
They are more than twelve. I want next
to carve King David, who wrote psalms and charms
we say daily for protection and
deliverance, to guide my father back.
But maybe not. That man danced and sang
and psalmed, but David was a king who sent
men from their homes and into war. I
might carve another soldier. The king of Prussia
and his captains would be pleased.

Do you know what they say about the bees,
that they guide each soul that floats towards heaven,
or towards hell? That's why we whisper names
to them, sweet emissaries who know this world
and eight others.
                        I say, small honeyling,
if you see my father, tell him all
is well with us, two grandsons and a small
granddaughter. Son and grandson carry on
his good, beloved name. But I tell
to this bee, mother's name,
name of his dear, departed wife.

WHY I DID NOT WANT TO BE A GIRL

When I was a boy I nailed
two-by-fours to elm trees, climbed

high, plunged my bike up
and over gravel piles the city crews

forgot when snow had melted,
explored the fetid creek that flowed

through culverts and the secret brickwork
cell beneath the street with iron

rungs that mounted toward the manhole,
discovered someone's secret stash of *Playboys*,

smoked Swisher Sweets, drank vodka
with Orange Crush and climbed the water

tower, falling only from the last three steps.
All ladders led in both directions,

all the answers simply yes or no,
and all bedrooms still seemed safe at night.

OF A FEATHER

My muse messaged last night that she'd moved again,
this time to New Mexico's high desert,
leaving me dangling to fill in her story.

I should tell you her tale, this fairy-tale woman,
absconding with faux fur white jacket,
the one with broad shoulders that nudges her ebony hair,
her cherry red lipstick. And the shoes!

She's really my opposite,
won't speak her own story.
I implore her to finish the manuscript,
but every labor of love gets rewritten, as if
how it happened was feeble,
and then the memories taint.

Her story has several components:
a mother, two fathers, sisters, brothers,
some boyfriends, calamitous substances,
all kinds of illness, unsuitable
husbands, ex-husbands, writers.

But there should be secrets, so maybe I'll leave out
the radio, the sexual ache,
the notes taped up all over the house,
reminders of clothes and not flying.

Maybe those signs could title her story;
we all like a title, a frame for our focus, something
that points to why. Goose down

could be another inscription—
I see her in feathers, or maybe that single,
long plume that dipped in front of her cloche hat,
as she sipped from her Slivovitz and sang in my ear
the song her Polish grandmother purred.

Or cities, I could name cities we've known, New
York, New Haven, Seattle, St. Paul, Minneapolis,
and now Dumbfuck, New Mexico?
I think I've forgotten some of the cities and some
of the exes, the stories are bleeding together;
it's been ten years since I saw her and still
she keeps moving around without telling me.

Two people who keep giving up
is one of the names of this poem.

Now I've lost the fairy tale thread but think
this is a fable where someone is boiled
or burned or buried alive
before the transfiguring roar.

She floats in on eiderdown;
I see her and think, where am I, standing
here with my longing, scrambled up
by the tall girls' steel wheels? She is someone
who knows how to remove herself.
She is someone who will not be still.

PRIMITIVE TOOLS

Stone and stone and stone am I,
without fur, not the strongest.
I am tracking what is missing,
hungry for the hard grain that sleeps still.

What does it take
to wake the icebound earth?

This slow stillness does not breathe;
the seed may never be born.
But I have learned to forge iron.
I have learned to make a knife.

I AM A BEAR

I am a bear, a mudhead climbing out of the earth;
I am a bear whose lips whisper this sonnet.

I am a bear, an animal with a bone between its legs;
I am a bear, mesmerizing with a well-trimmed beard and dark eyes.

Come, look at my loosening robe
and run your hands through my glistening fur.

I am a bear, and will tell you how Rapunzel became my mother;
I am a bear; Vladimir Putin has nothing to do with me.

I am a bear, the wolves smell me coming;
I am a bear, given to dreaming when love mutters its howl.

I am a bear, my pinkness sweetens with honey;
I am a bear: my tongue is salted with black ants.

STONES FOR CROSSING A RIVER OR STREAM

They are irregular, with sloping sides
and delicate moss, slimy and trailing
in water, like fine hair
that smears in the palm of my hand.

The stones are never spaced right.
I must have started on the wrong foot,
left for right, right for left:
mud below, and an unknown current.

I am a fool for perching on this rock,
and I am a fool for not perching
on this rock.
I accept that a foot will get wet.

But how can I cherish these slippery stones
distant as stars in the dark?
How can I wake to and bless these hard shapes
that stand as the waters wash by?

OLD MAN BEAR SONG

I say these things that you might see them,
I love these things that you might love them.

I sing pale birches in the summer,
glowing in their heavy forest,

petals going green to gold,
and pearly bark joined with the stars,

so birch becomes a full-moon tree
and rests between the two great wheels.

I say these things that you might see them,
I love these things that you might love them.

I chant of pine in winter whiteness,
fragrant green boughs with ice blossoms,

dark bark of spruce marks every ridge,
holds out cold arms, green needle packets.

The lines on birch mark lidded eyes,
while snow falls soft from heavy skies,

Wood warms me as I rest this body,
as I stretch beneath eight blankets of snow.

I say these things that you might see them,
I love these things that you might love them.

WITCH TREE, LAKE SUPERIOR

The Witch Tree stands on its granite north shore,
a cedar that's clung over three hundred years.
It hangs over water, a battered old crone,
and lives through strange fissures and crevices.

A cedar on stone over three hundred years
that's painted and pictured because it can't last,
it lives through strange fissures and crevices.
I'd like to interview one of its limbs,

or paint or record it because it can't last,
or ask its inner ear how to survive.
I'd like to interview one of its limbs
and ask how to balance.

I'd ask its inner ear how we survive.
I saw the X-ray of my neck (the cervical vertebrae),
and asked how to balance,
why bone migrates from jaw to lymph node.

I saw the X-ray of my neck (the cervical vertebrae)
(the hair on my head grows thinner and finer):
I asked why bone migrates from jaw to lymph node.
I never expected a cloud to carry so much rain.

The hair on my head grows thinner and finer.
An oriole works on a nest of old horsehair and sticks.
The dark thundercloud carries just so much rain,
and the grass has lived here thousands of years.

The oriole works on a nest of old horsehair and sticks,
a tree on the north shore is called the Witch Tree,
and grass roots have lived here thousands of years,
caressing these rocks like battered old crones.

IT IS CALLED A TRACERY

I.

Twining the top of a window,
branching beyond and above,
carved in stone, in wood,
splaying like shadows of tree limbs in winter,

it casts a pattern,
a shadow, on promises, plans, spirit blessings,
work that still threads my thoughts
into a thicket, benedictions and creeds,

chant and enchantment sung in slow notes under pillars like trees,
weaving regrets and forsaking, querulous barbs,
the dimness of days that darken my thoughts, noise of hymns sung
with eyes full of tears so heavy the pages were blurred,

and the infinite number of thoughts twigging forward.
It shades a sung word, daring, imperious to breathe,
the sung word, the stem of an oak,
each multiplied branch making it taller and stronger,

drawing me closer, before the escape flows past me,
a woman, who glimpsed lakes over treetops,
who dreamed a dark horse could waft her away.
I fling myself at the roots of this tree, my face in the soil,

consumed by words and the study of signs,
scouring for one common atom uniting it all,
loving the unseen, invisible world,
holding fast to the blossoming tree limbs.

2.

In the cathedral,
when sun shifts north, melting the ice and the snow,
in the chancel with carved wooden choir stalls,
the choir sounds warm, *a capella*.

Soprano and tenor float above alto and bass,
each part beginning, then picked up by another,
a marvelous fabric of sound mixed with words,
yet no words for the sound they create.

I in my bench imagine my song with them,
throat opening full, lungs filling with air, expelling again and again;
the air comes in from the space, nourishing,
then a part escapes to join other breaths, the invisible body.

Creating God, your fingers trace. . .
Seven whole days, not one in seven, I will praise thee. . .
I bind unto myself today. . .

3.

Then swift, the magic breaks,
the promise of blended voices building together proves false,
harmony an illusion when shouting shows strength,
all my words taken away.

Christ be with me, Christ within me, Christ behind me, Christ before me,
Christ beside me, Christ to win me, Christ to comfort and restore me. . .

There is no comfort here
as we perch on our velvet benches, listening, straining,
the melodies circling in unstable harmonies,
the suspended fourth tone that defies resolution.

The note leads me out,
into the vibrant wood grain of the bench,
the image of lapping waves and eddies
each moment the tree grew still taller.

It draws me out like the dark horse that danced in my dreams,
beside me always, leaping the ditches and road signs,
its long, tangled mane that turned in its wake
like leaves in a sudden, strong wind.

4.

. . . by invocation of the same, the Three in One, and One in Three,
Of whom all nature hath creation. . .

The sound washes wonder over me
as light glints through windows,
the metal and stonework pointed and curving,
dividing the segments of light like the horse's dark legs

that carry the child where her heart must lead,
to the boll of the oak, a bundle of dappling twigs and boughs,
planting itself even as it rots inside,
replenishing even as it is cut down.

You branches,
your echoes and turns that I follow
alone with my tiny bract off the main shoot,
I long for your lift and your shelter.

5.

The leaves make a sound, a washing, a river of breath.
They answer each other without hesitation
as they turn in the wind and grow against gravity, murmuring,
break, break, break, break,

like a plainchant the horse hears and stands still for,
and the choir sings to the light,
break, break, break, break,
and I open my mouth to echo the sound

and see as I finger the grain of wood making its river,
a thousand dark horses next to the stream,
each dipping its long head to drink from the water,
each one coming out from a thicket of sharp stems like thorns.

THE KEY TO MY HOUSE

How to begin?

I remember Rice Krispies, Cheerios,
Wheaties, Special K;
their light cardboard boxes
kept under the counter
next to the coffee,
electric fry pan,
and yellow and red bucket of lard.

Don't misunderstand.
I don't see these
at the breakfast table.
I don't need milk
and a melamine bowl
for these flavors.

Back then I carried a house key, gold,
one end like a clover leaf,
hung on green string.

Once a boy stole it.

Of course he was teasing.
He thought it was jewelry,
a good-luck charm.

That was when I was twelve.
I'd been carrying that key
since second grade.

I carried that key
thirty years more
until someone stole
my whole purse.

I must get back to the food.

Every day I'd let myself in, drop
a satchel of books and my violin
next to the armchair
then walk to the kitchen
and bathe in the bulb
of the open refrigerator,
wondering what I could pilfer
that would not be missed.

I'd grab a chunk of Colby cheese
and the slicer,
head back to the living room
and turn on the TV.
Slice by slice—
was I measuring time?
No one would be home for hours.

The gold hands of the clock
over the piano
hummed electrically forward—
slice, slice, slice,
3:20, 3:25, 3:45,
until the inside of my mouth
felt slick and slow with cold milk-fat
and I got up to look
for another texture
to roll onto my tongue.

The idea was to not noticeably
deplete resources.
That's probably why
I sometimes stopped
filching from cereal boxes
found under the counter,
carrying them to the living room
where I'd watch TV and stick
my calloused small hand
in the wax paper liner
and heft handfuls of dry cereal
into my mouth.

I grazed everywhere, on everything edible,
the gooey, crystalline-dried ice melt
on the inside lids of old ice cream
in the basement freezer,
a few frozen blueberries.

Seldom-used things dwelled in the pantry—
seldom-used food.

How can I describe our lives then?
My parents saved and reused everything.

Brown sugar got hard,
one of the confectioner's sugar bags
leaked. The Uncle Ben's Rice
must have been left over from when
my brother went to Korea
or Idaho, or wherever
they stationed him.

Inside a cabinet door with a black knob
and glass that was wavy and bubbled
stood ambition—red hots
for cookies, sprinkles for cupcakes,
currants for gingerbread men.

For baking, small amber bottles
of flavors—lemon extract, orange,
vanilla, and almond.
I'd heard about extracts.

I'd unscrew a diminutive red cap
and lift the phial to my lips.
The flavors tasted like fire.

Each time I visited
these 160-proof extracts,
I took care to hold up each bottle
against the small pantry window,
and note where the liquid
held to the label.

With these,
I was careful.
I couldn't sip often.
I kept looking for food.

Two bags of marshmallows,
already open, hard and chewy,
like dense meringues,
pushed back on a pantry shelf.

I still prefer them that way.

For months I watched
an unopened Rice Krispies box
lodged sideways on an open pantry shelf,
above canned tomatoes and green beans.
When I read its expiration date
(more than a year past),
I triumphantly pulled the box from its tomb
and carried it to the living room
where I watched *Dark Shadows*.

My mother scolded me
for eating the ingredients
she'd planned to use to make
Rice Krispie bars.
When? I stormed,
and pointed out the expiration date.

This was one of many bouts
in which I'd learn my logic
was not welcome.

My mother tried to do it all,
and unmade Rice Krispie bars
were her breaking point.

But that's another poem.

ONE LAST QUESTION
For Jon Bailey

He asks, *Is it peaceful or quiet?*
A droll philosophical challenge

in a florescent aisle of cubicles, bereft
of their code-writing tenants, except for us now,

and soon just me left at my desk. I know
what he means as he lingers a moment,

but don't know that this is our last
conversation, our riddling, final good-bye.

I ponder his question, knowing peace parallels calm,
an absence of stress, banal interruptions,

and quiet means lonely—everyone absent,
solitary confinement.

I am typing again when I wave
him away from my doorway

because I want to hold planets
in orbits and don't even know why.

Then hospital, emergency gurney,
and his heart . . . heart . . . heart . . .

I search for a different word, a name
given to ground when it buckles and settles

to untimely ruins lying still in prone,
scattered shapes. Yes, friend, this is quiet.

THE GREENING

I stand behind my house,
holding a small sledge hammer,
and wonder what I should hit next.

Sweat greases my forehead and chin,
raising colonies of angry red bumps.
I will not think of that now.

I am twenty-seven. My long, dirty-blond
hair rainbows with fuchsia extensions
(fused with glue guns back then in the eighties).

It's shaved to dark stubble just over
my left ear, and when people ask,
sometimes I tell them I burned that part off.

I'm wearing my black Eraserhead t-shirt.
This is before I've said much
to Gladys, born in the house next door

82 years ago. We've waved over the chain
link fence that went up sometime
between my touring this house

and the day I moved in. I squint
in the alkaline glare of concrete,
my new back yard, an old parking

slab for six cars. I swing
at a longish point of cement
that looks ready to crack.

Gladys watches me now
on my rubble-strewn stage.
My wrists shudder each time

the sledge head connects with its target,
but I'm going to get this job done
with whatever tools I can find.

Some of my hair wanders into my mouth
as I shovel up grapefruit-sized concrete chunks
and drop them into a little red wagon.

I'll never know when she left her post
at the window, but when she looked out
again and saw green sod where drum fires

had flared, she understood
someone new had moved in next door.
She invited me into her house

and showed me her scrapbooks. I admired
her small grand piano and told her
about my plans for the gardens.

She stood up and walked to the kitchen,
opened a drawer, and gave me
her brother-in-law's spare billy club.

APOGEE

I lift the iron latch
to open the gate

and let the night
air flow down the hill,

the star-filled sky
splashing across familiar

darkness, with so much
unfamiliar light, glinting

particles, larger distant blazing
beacons, gleaming sky krill,

fantastic, bold, luminous,
slow raindropped gems suspended

in dawn day morning spider
webs, shimmering, catching

light, making light,
distant sources of all light,

no impediments, no dark
mountain, but all fabric, visible

and hidden, all unseen, availing;
unnamed constellations hold

my hands, my fingers, grasp
my ankles, touch each metatarsal,

buss each eyelid, press and part my lips,
and sky swallows me into its hot, bright night.

IF SOMEWHERE

If somewhere a horned owl clings to the pine,
cleaning sharp claws, unfurling her wings,

if somewhere Beethoven broods over tallow,
pushing his pen toward an augmented sixth,

if somewhere a blizzard falls into an ocean
descending in crystals that kiss fins of sea bass,

if somewhere the citizens hear the last bell
of a carillon ringing at noon in the square,

then love with its patient eyes and warm hands
will walk up a mountain and stand at your door,

and loosen its shoelaces on the door mat,
and quietly listen for your quickening steps.

How long it has stood there and when it might leave
is something not even a shaman can guess,

yet here is its shadow and here is its tread;
and here is its suitcase, and here is its breath.

HOW WE LOVE

(in homage to Marianne Moore)

You have to be willing to bend, to test each
       new kind of posture,
             to supplicate,
                   kneeling,
     to brandish an eye

for each fragment—you have to admit that the
       stately procession
             of lush grass spears
                 clusters
     and builds a new lawn—

you have to admire the bird that swings through
       leafless pear branches,
             tilting her head,
                 sensing,
     finding fat wood wasps—

you must wear hats and coil your hair, divine
       strength in compression,
             the animal
                 curled in
           its straw-feathered nest,

quiet armor of spine: then you will see with
       available light,
             into "a place
                 that only
   feet can enable."

DECEMBER, 1967

What you loved most about the Christmas tree
was lying underneath it on your back.
You loved staring through the branches
at the colored lights made larger
by their tin reflectors and short bristling needles
sprucing up the house with outdoor smells,
calmed, while loud voices floated over you,
invisible, small child beneath a tree.

When you weren't underneath the tree
by its picture window
you fiddled with the pixie angel
made from green pipe cleaners
and the clown, tufted red and white,
flying them from tree to window sill and cave
beneath the radiator where the cat could hide.

Better not to make noise,
not be spied.

You learned how not to be an obstacle,
how to clean a room, leave no trace of yourself,
how to hide, and sink into a book.
You watched images of space, the final frontier,
and later listened to the songs of Major Tom,
the one who floated far above the world,
and found his own place in the starry, lovely lights.

GEOMANCER

Go to the church of tall trees
to build a house, watch wind and weather.
Roots will appear in strange places,
and cradle the turf.

Tell me about the symmetry of rooms,
and describe your beloved's face,
high cheek bones constant,
the soul's windows open and equal.

Listen to rocks,
press temple and cheek to cool roughness,
ear cupping a seashell of sound
that composes a lifeboat, a keen hawk

that circles the sky. Gather the roots
like a tree that swirls from its base,
the rivened tree trunk, also collect
smooth pieces of wood like bone.

Pass time in this space,
glide by mathematical windows,
rooms of Masonic dimensions,
the sun always rising, the east.

Love windows more than the furniture,
live in the attic, an elegant crow's nest
of angles that open and close.
You like your lines clean. They all add up.

A SUPERMARKET IN MINNESOTA

Some time after midnight (rock and roll shopping) at Rainbow
Uptown (Mistress Jean, aisle six, in a catsuit),

next to the shelves of canned goods a woman with wavy brown hair
smiled at you and you smiled back because you thought she liked you,

then she stepped forward to say her prayer group had just read the article,
were praying that you would accept Jesus, get on the right path, and not change
    God's will.

Some admire your music, some think you are brave
for publically being transgender. Others pray.

You don't like to argue, especially with strangers in grocery aisles,
so you reached to the back of the shelf, feeling around for tomato puree,

while her terror of hell if she didn't save someone heat-sparked the overhead
    lights.
You nodded and mentally chanted, *I am a whole person, not broken,*

only later beginning to grasp your prayer was for both of you, after you found
the 39-cent can of mushroom pieces and stems and settled it into the well of
    your cart.

SANDRA BLAND, SANDRA BLAND, WHERE IS YOUR SOUL AFTER YOUR TRAFFIC STOP IN PRAIRIE VIEW, TEXAS, AND MYSTERIOUS DEATH IN JAIL?

only your lissome
for love
lacerations
      you are a

small child of round song
the Spirit of God
a taser
      and lips

you have a
dwelleth within you
twisted
      for the temple

knee to neck
of God
O just so *holy*
      is someone recording

you are
with a season
sharp turn
      Alleluia

you have
of whom ye do
last cigarette
      this day celebrate

you hang
joys of the temple
tailing
      your body

which temple
this road stop
Behold
      dream-schooled

your eye   apt pupil
you oubliette *tabernacle*
of God chanting covered with
      eyes front and back

LITTLE

Yesterday your boyfriend threw the small boy
and kicked his ribs
and his small head

The eyelids
still
fluttering

That was too much
for one
day

*

Do you want a bed
a quilt to cover up
the night

to take away the chill,
to wrap around
your neck?

The flowers in the shade are budded white

but shrivel
in dry soil

If there were only one flower still in bloom

*

Two ears for hearing
but the left one
rings

Two eyes for sealing
shut

The spark
is colorless
before it

disappears

Gas-scented
soot exhaust

Each shortened breath

Each little press
of lungs

THERE IS NO CURE

There is no cure for marriage. It's how
we find ourselves inside a sudden gust that blows
the portals open, far from balance,

like when a thirteen-year-old girl slams shut
the storm door and her father watches all its shattered
glass fall out and her mother swallows hard into a knot.

I ran away to school one day and then returned to find
the glass made whole again. No one said a word.

Say you've been a child who slammed a door,
or opened up a wound, say that when you shout
another voice will likely shout back even louder.

This fevered thing reminds you who you always were,
a wishful thinker, planner, dreamer, lover
of the latent stampede, hungry for the gallop,

cruel to use your teeth to send a message,
force attention, nip loved ones from straying:
ravenous, and wrong to use your mouth.

WHEN WE HAD HOOVES

What are these words for,
I ask you, love, my changing star.

Three decades ago you said,
You can't be an artist
if you're not painting; you can't be
a writer if you're not writing, you can't
be a dancer if you're not dancing,
as we bumped down the highway
in the '78 brown Renault,
back bumper replaced by a bolted
steel bar, ugly but practical, one
of the unsaid economies of art.

We were consumed by galloping
ideas nothing could stop.

Another car conversation:
I lay under it with you, the engine
chained above, and I helped you
position the tiny gear pins that only my
small hands could hang onto.

The conversations we had
about art, about music—you said
art was religion, and I went
to that church, knelt,
and folded my hands.

When did you stop climbing

through windows of abandoned
old warehouses to photograph dead wings
left behind? When did you stop
winding your old Bolex camera in circles
around Jim Morrison's grave?

Whose horse will come apart first, head
detached from its body,
skull washed clean
of all color and meat?

I dream of a horse
head nailed to the gate
that sings out the truth.

Where is your horse in this?

When we lay under the car,
wondering if the beam
that held up the 400-pound engine
was strong enough, we both
rolled on the concrete and laughed.

The idea of working
beneath all that weight
and still being alive.

NO BREATH, NO BODY

late that summer I helped
a friend inseminate
her horse, with semen
I picked up in a large blue
bucket from the airport
super-cooled from California
not frozen

while all that year I paid
a grim-faced doctor
who scowled
at my transgender spouse
who said my womb
was never "challenged"
with a sperm

month after month he watched
while his assistant poked
a plastic tube between
my legs
clamping the end until
my body cramped
and shivered with the pain

the mare formed a foal
while I formed nothing
but a loss
of something that never
existed, a thin line in a test kit
that never
appeared

RHUBARB

We will start by digging a rhubarb vineyard:
rhubarb, because nothing can kill it.

We will plant rhubarb crowns, hairy rootlets
with pale bulging skin, tough enough to survive 30 below.

The plot in warm sun will not stink of dogs,
it will not smell of a sewer, or athletic cheese of the body.

When the neighbors built a two-car garage over their garden,
rhubarb's elephant leaves still burst from the concrete foundation.

So we plunge trowels into dirt and hoist clumps of foil,
ripped red-checked cardboard, chicken wing bones,

whiskey glass, scrape dirt away from a Bakelite
piece of a rotary phone, a radio dial and slide.

A vegetable kingdom is rising over the rubble,
over paint chips and plastic pill bottle caps.

The rhubarb sets in, gripping its earthy mélange;
blind digging in darkness to extract its chthonian vintage.

BEFORE I DO ANYTHING ELSE

I must tell you the world is round, it folds fragments together,
ingredients stirred in a bowl, then expands,

and you are my luscious raisin or olive
or fig fruit pushed away as the dough rises.

I hear you type in the next room,
fingers pausing then pounding the keys.

I plot my course to look for your gaze
and pass through the garden to see which plants

made it through drought, which ones droop
and languish for rain.

Their posture does not show it,
but even the upright plants thirst.

NO, I'LL MILK THE REINDEER

I'd like bills to be paid & I'd like
to stop hearing & feeling the chaos of
caring & cleaning up after others   it
takes too much from my life   messes
choke me like weeds & I'll never get
any writing done when I keep solving
problems for others but it's easier
for me to just do it & then everyone goes
to bed early or wakes up late & I'm limping
up and down stairs on two sprained ankles
& this can't be good for my health   I know
stress leads to dementia & is proven to shrink
women's brains & I need my brain   it's
what I make my living with   it's what I live
life with & my doctor asked if I'd had
mood changes & no I'm just tired
& yes I swore & I stomped when someone
took the whole pad of Post-its I hid in the
cupboard & now they are lost & I am the
only one keeping track of numbers like
$22,400   18-24-14   888-525-1237   2354 &
if I lived circa 1200 I'd be crouched by a
fire & make sure to spin all the wool by late
winter   I'd be ready for weaving & planting
& tending of spring & chanting a song to
help it along & I'd count the spools & the hides
& watch the dwindling food & admonish
the men drinking tea to go out & bring back
more animals & no you may not open a new
pouch of food before this last one is done & no

I'll milk the reindeer   I know how to stop
her from kicking the bowl   if you want more
milk get me a goat or even a cow & you better
get someone else to help with that bear.

FOR YOUR INFORMATION

Today I found
your discarded banana peel
in the basement
on top of the dryer
removable lint trap
and realized

I must incite disorder.

So you will find
your blackening peel
on the kitchen counter,
tented like a tiny bath cabana
where you may undress
and dive headlong,
swim toward your hidden treasures
in the laundry room
among pleasant-scented cleaning supplies.

As you nose your way
past green-blue grottoes
you may see me
settled in one,
leaning forward,
word-smitten,
chewing on a bookmark.

Please do not interrupt me;
I am working.
Wave if you must.

EVERY ASTONISHING DAY OF MY LIFE

1.

I was six when I wrote my first story
about a cat and a dog who fell
in love and married and birthed
a puppy and kitten.

At ten I could have married a horse,
at thirteen I heard David Bowie
and went interplanetary.
At sixteen I still kissed my horse.

I dated artists, musicians. At eighteen
I loved a man with long red hair
who played guitar, who was too shy
to speak. I read our tarot cards.

I married him. We played like puppies,
we played like kittens, we dressed like punks,
and when I was twenty-eight
he wanted to be a woman.

2.

Two-spirited person, this *they* that I loved,
hadn't grown up like a girl,
but this was their inland sea,
where the canals of their brain led.

I got on the train,
I screamed at band members,
I held down the fort,
I started going to church.

When I was forty-three we argued.
No money, no patience, we blew up
at a funeral, we could never love
as much as those two loved. We parted.

No one else understood me. Saw me.
Or rarely. But still. Everything.
Becomes.
I welcomed my love back.

3.

 What are we doing to each other and why
do I love one who so confounds me?
I hear the sough of your breath
as you lie dreaming of all your disasters.

I married confusion, I sought
everything and its opposite.
I still read the paper to see
small stories unfolding in corners.

I still sit at the table. I still leave
out significant parts of my story, my sins.
I still marry my strange familiar
every astonishing day of my life.

KISS

This kiss lives by its own
rules, with its whinny,
its mini hello to connect
and enthrall as it noses,
supposes some prize,
tries to taste with its teeth, tongue,
pink lapper, flung hunger,
its wildfire choir,
its open-mouthed
amen.

MY GRANDMOTHER DREAMS
OF THE FINNISH TANGO

They began practicing after she left
because war sundered the world
and dance warmed their bodies.
Her sister wrote with the news: Argentine travelers,
red roses swaddled with reindeer robes:
all hearts beat faster, faster.

She could see it, feel it, heat,
and wanted to tuck her chin into his body,
imagined their legs, gliding, lovely, parallel strides, skis,
love-making vertical, a new longitude,
the music so natural it wept in the wind
whistling past her milk house.

Her sister said they sang tangos of love, of sorrow,
or a distant land of happiness.
She was in that distant land of happiness, chipping ice
off the milk pail again; the man she loved with strong shoulders
shoveled a path through the snow to the road,
so their children could ride to a school with strange language.

Why did she leave? When she called for her children,
they answered to new, American names. Her friends
would not recognize her brow, heavy waist,
her rough, farmwife hands still longing
to hold a young man so tall and light on his feet,
so easy to follow and dance with.

THE PROTOCOL

It was below zero when they started for home.
Their headlights caught fingers of snow as it blew
across blacktop from dormant acres of soy fields.
He was driving her car, so she should remind him

about gas, which made her remember if he made
more money, the gauge would be fixed by now.
But she was good at calculating (wasn't that
how they survived?), and there had to be

at least 60 miles left in the tank.
But they should buy more, which reminded her
that he was the kind of man to take
an inconvenient request as an insult,

which meant she spoke in a voice
calibrated by decades of chafing, which meant
it emerged like a bleat (she hated that),
which meant he mildly listened, then

went back to describing the fish and the cat,
which amused her, which meant they both missed the turn
for the station. No worry, she said, there'd be
a chance once they got on the freeway, and after

a while she asked for the name of the fish
again, and he wondered if they could get
one like that (Zippy, the koi with orange dot),
then the motor stumbled

a step, and he looked at her and shrugged,
so she shrugged back, and a few miles later
it choked and stopped, which sounded a lot
like the time the fuel pump went.

Still, they had phones. Both of them tapped
their buttons and passwords, first she, then he,
finding themselves in a dead spot. She wondered
how many miles had passed since that station.

He wondered, were there farmhouses or cabins?
People were warned to stay with their cars
in this kind of emergency. But he had to get out
to open the hood, and she got out too,

to check on the wind and her door blew
out wide to the side. She scrabbled forward,
stood next to him, hands hovering for warmth
over the cooling mass of the engine.

KIND-HEARTED MONSTER

One expects a plant to have root
or attachment,
but after that, almost any
thing can happen.

For a picture, draw a stick,
topped with scalloping flower, add
a single leaf that juts out at the side.
Mother's elbow.

That does not begin
to describe how pineapples
in their beds of aloe spears,
their myriads of thorny eyes

winking as they rise,
open spiked, tufted crowns
where they prepare to birth
sweet new juicy hand grenades,

or how arteries of mushrooms
branch the underworld tracing
rotting roots of distant cousins,
trees, their forage.

Observe scars of tomatoes
that strap and bind like knots
a dominatrix ties
around her client's scrotum,

how inner tension pushes all
the fruit's meat out, how pressure
pulls it tight, how its skin expands.
And then how it shines.

READING THE PETROGLYPHS AT JEFFERS

Red, holy island rising from oceans of grass,
red rock of memory that breaches the prairie,

holy the four and six points marking all space
holy the spirits here mingled with stone,

holy the visions and wishes drawn near,
holy their breaths passing through rock.

All the swift animals have circular feet;
they die and they come back again and again.

The bird that makes thunder walks on the earth
and shows his strong heart to all who walk here—

bear, elk, and buffalo—while a two-legged form
bends and opens her supplicant hands.

Holy the place where all the stars turn,
their quiet light pushing the wheel of the sky.

THE THING ABOUT THE OCEAN

A man walks into the ocean.
His feet churn clouds of sand,
waves fall against the verge.

The shoreline gives and takes,
it takes in water, ocean draws it back,
draws sand away from shore.

A man who walks into the ocean will try
to count the waves, mark every seventh wave,
and might lose track, so he stops awhile.

Any man walking into the ocean is amalgamated;
kelp quivers on the sandy floor, seaweed
tendrils snake by, sailboats, fish boats, yachts.

This man walks into the ocean and feels waves slap
against his thighs, he stoops to bring the water
to his chest. The next wave comes, his feet lift.

A man in the ocean sees the ferry offshore,
he thinks of things that live below the surface,
how they bring the bodies home.

A man who walks into the ocean is a body,
and water touches everything,
a concentration, salt and brine,

to make things float. It breathes, it heaves
against land. Wave after wave pulls,
then returns the revenant buoyant to shore.

THE TREES SPEAK SO PLAINLY AT PIKE ISLAND, AN INTERNMENT CAMP WINTER 1862-1863 FOR DAKOTA WOMEN, CHILDREN, AND ELDERS

These trees know the chill of an island, its dampness;
they've given their galls in memory of people
taken away from their home, their *makha*,
cut so keenly it must have stung like a knife.

Beneath all the murmured prayers for safe landings
as jet after jet glides over the brooding expanse
of two rivers, a mighty confluence
coursing around this small island,

beneath Mendota Bridge where a vanishing point
on the opposite bank perches hundreds of feet
above islets of scrub trees, I can't comfort a soul.
I stand on the shore and look

at the flickering water with curious snags,
the island an arrow point.
The trees speak so plainly.
Would I save anyone?

There's no honest answer. I've made terrible
errors in judgment; I've done a good job
of saving my own skin. I shiver to read
the messages knotted in each canted branch.

BEATITUDE FOR KEVIN BRIXIUS

Blessed the bicycle, as cheap as a thumb, and the bus ride through Turkey,
     the language of face, hands, and feet;

blessed the wheels of the cities, cracked concrete, flowers that grow in the
     sidewalks and stoops;

blessed the birds that sing in small maples along Third Avenue;

blessed strong taproots of dandelions, mothers, sleepless, smoothing their
     hair, and teenagers tuning guitar strings;

blessed the big green booth, microphones, cords that don't buzz, Melissa
     your bartender;

blessed the rails and roads, rattling buses and cars, city parks, softball, beer,
     cigarettes, marijuana, bandanas;

blessed the ride from the highway, gravel road, thistle and mullein,
     the shade of a tree, rain, a tent, kerosene, coffee;

blessed the prairies, all bodies of water, small towns, forests, farmsteads, the
     smell of a cow, some chickens;

blessed the arm-shattering hayfields, the dust, moving metal, the nests of
     birds, wild kittens;

blessed the toddlers who shriek, they scour the beach, flatten every sand
     castle;

blessed the children who dodge, run past adult drinks, plates, fire, and when
        asked how wild they are, on a scale one to ten, rotate their arms to
        oblivion;

blessed that man struggling up from his chair, aged, light-headed, he's
        passed out four times this year;

blessed the preacher who quotes Black Elk, *birds make their nests in circles,*
        for theirs is the same religion as ours, at his young brother's funeral;

blessed that brother, Kevin, parking his car on a street blocks away from the
        hospital, hoping to save some money;

blessed the naked dreams, exposing the shame, the sciatica, shaving away
        pubic hair and still retaining the body;

blessed the years, weeks, days, and the hours, the cardinal numbers
        attached, measures of passage on earth and the wheeling away;

blessed the light, it brightens and pulses, it pedals away, blinks, heads down-
        hill, it disappears into dark.

THAT SINGING VOICE

In the hall notes sound, and artists and writers, musicians and lawyers, shop
       runners, carpenters, bartenders, bikers, grandmothers on dates, the nail-
       trimmers and benders, all ones who wish they could sing like that stop,
       all the talk stops, all the place listens:

all hear the deep well of voice filling up space, up forty feet, it touches the fixtures,
       it smokes the tin ceiling;

each longing ear hears a song that flows upward and vibrates a breastbone, a
       wing-bone, a wish-bone;

each longing body that cannot move like a bird's still shudders and opens for air,
       wings expanding the chest, building a timbre, a forest, a cradle;

each longing vessel cleaves kinship to rivers that carve through the hardness,
       through granite, through sandstone, through layers of limestone, through
       shale, pushing aside all the riprap,

each longing creature, each not-hollow instrument, knows palpitations of sounds
       moving through, the shiver that lingers, that reshapes its refuge;

each person senses how wood feels when it becomes violin, oboe, the echo of
       space inside a guitar, sounding board, touching drum skin, connected to
       ribs, or a tibia turned into flute, fingers all spreading, all bone, one way or
       another,

all scaffold to shelter the invisible blossom, human and breaking and beating
       within.

ACKNOWLEDGMENTS AND NOTES

Grateful thanks go to the many individuals who encouraged me and gave me feedback on these poems, most notably Kara Garbe Balcerzak, Kris Bigalk, Anthony Ceballos, Josh Cook, Natalie Diaz, Amy Fladeboe, Jonathon Heide, Melody Heide, Deborah Keenan, James Lenfestey, Rachel Nevins, Marie Olofsdotter, Kari Tauring, and Cary Waterman.

"Figurative Beehives, Upper Silesia" refers to a 16th to 18th century European tradition of carving beehives into Biblical and familiar cultural figures. Several eight-foot tall examples of these can be found at the Ethnographic Museum in Wroclaw, Poland. The last section of the poem refers to the Euro-Celtic folk tradition of telling the bees that someone has died.

"For Your Information" appeared in *Green Hills Literary Lantern*, volume 27, 2016.

"How We Love" contains a quotation in the last section from *The Old Ways: A Journey on Foot*, by Robert MacFarlane (Penguin, 2012).

"If Somewhere" appeared in *Alligator Juniper*, volume 21, spring 2017.

"It Is Called a Tracery" appeared in *Seminary Ridge Review*, autumn 2015.

"Kind-Hearted Monster" was inspired by a painting of the same name by Asuka Hishiki.

"Listening to the Songs of the French Voyageurs While I Float in My Mother's Womb" was inspired by a true story about a little boy in Massachusetts trans-fixed by a stranger's North Carolina accent. It turned out to be the accent of his birth mother. Since then I have come across several studies indicating that babies recognize voices and songs they originally heard in utero.

"Primitive Tools" appeared in the great weather for MEDIA anthology, *Before Passing*, 2015.

"Sandra Bland, Sandra Bland" refers to Sandra Bland, a young African-American woman who was pulled over and dubiously arrested at a traffic stop in Waller County, Texas, July 10th, 2015. The disturbing dashcam video of the traffic incident went viral. Three days later, she was found hanging in her jail cell. The italicized lines are from the choral anthem "Behold, the Tabernacle of God," composed by William Harris.

"Stones for Crossing a River or Stream" appeared in *Green Hills Literary Lantern*, volume 27, 2016.

"The Thing about the Ocean" appeared in slightly different form in *The River Muse*, March 2013.

ABOUT THE AUTHOR

LYNETTE REINI-GRANDELL is also the author of *Approaching the Gate* (Holy Cow! Press, 2014), which won the Northeastern Minnesota Book Award for Poetry. Her work has been nominated for a Pushcart Prize and is part of a permanent art installation at the Carlton Arms Hotel in Manhattan. She has received grants from the Finlandia Foundation and the Minnesota State Arts Board and holds an MA and PhD in literature from the University of Minnesota. A two-time president of the Minnesota Council of Teachers of English, she teaches at Normandale Community College. She lives in Minneapolis, where she reads regularly with the Bosso Poetry Company, performs with the jazz/poetry collective Sonoglyph, and is married to the transgender performance artist/musician, Venus de Mars. More information is available on her website, *www.Reini-Grandell.com.*